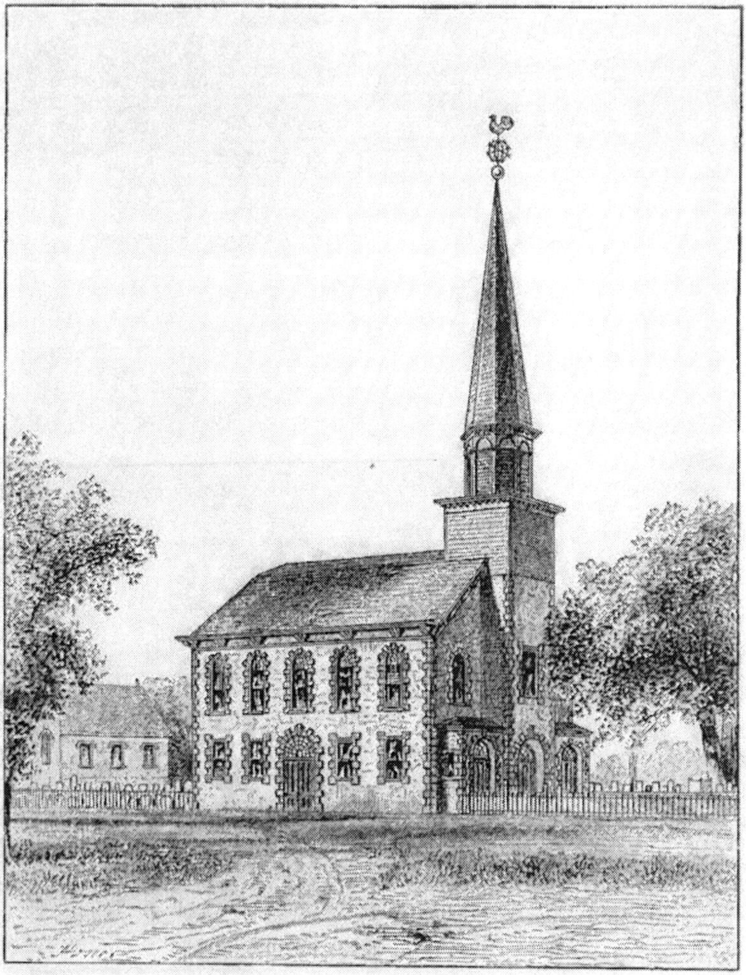

THE FIRST REFORMED DUTCH CHURCH.—FISHKILL VILLAGE.

Tombstone Inscriptions

FROM

THE CHURCHYARD OF THE

First Reformed Dutch Church

OF

FISHKILL VILLAGE, DUTCHESS CO., N. Y.

COMPILED BY

E. W. VAN VOORHIS
OF NEW YORK CITY

FOR PRIVATE DISTRIBUTION ONLY

Press of
G. P. Putnam's Sons
New York

INTRODUCTION.

The earliest historical reference to the First Reformed Dutch Church of Fishkill Village, is found in the third volume of the Documentary History of New York, page 589, where the following paper is recorded:

" Petition for aid to erect a church at Fish creek, Dutchess Co.

To His Excellency John Montgomerie Esqr. Capt. Generall and Governor in Chief in and over his Majesties' Provinces of New York and New Jersey and the Territories depending thereon in America, and Vice Admirall of the same &c

The humble Petition of Peter Du Bois and Abraham Musy, Elders, and Abraham Blinkerhof and Hendrick Phillips, Deacons, of the Dutch Reformed Protestant Church of the fish Creek in Dutchess County in the Province of New York in behalf of themselves and the Rest of the members of the said Church

Humbly Sheweth

That the members of the said Congregacon, being in daily expectation of a minister from hol-
land to preach the Gospel amongst them ac-
cording to the Cannons, Rules and Discipline
of the Reformed Protestant Churches of the
united Netherlands, and therefore have agreed
amongst themselves to erect and build a Con-
veniant Church for the Publick worship of God,
nigh the said fish creek in the County aforesaid,
but finding that the said building will be very
Chargeable, and therefore as in the like cases
has been Practised and is usuall in this Province
they would desire the aid and help and assist-
ance of all Charitable and well disposed Chris-
tians within this Province for the Compleating
of the said Building

They therefore most humbly Pray for your
Excellency's Lycence to be granted to the said
Elders and Deacons of the said Protestant Congregacon to collect gather and Receive the
benevolence and free gifts of all such Inhabitants
of this Province as shall be willing to contribute
somewhat toward the erecting and building
such Church as aforesaid for the Publick service
of almighty God, and that only for such time as

your Excellency will be pleased to grant the said Lycence,

in behalf of the Elders and Deacons and other the members of said Congregacon

28th June 1731. PITER DU BOIS."

T. Van Wyck Brinckerhoff, Esq., in his historical sketch of Fishkill states "that although the building of the church is not positively stated in the above petition, yet in a certain bond bearing date the same year it is clearly stated that they ' had agreed and built a church,' and that there was a Glebe attached to the Church, which Glebe land was purchased in two different lots —one containing seven and almost one-half acres was purchased from Madame Brett—the other portion ' containing three quarters of an acre and fifteen rods with the appurtenances whereon to erect a church or house for the service or worship of them, in manner and form as aforesaid, for the inhabitants of the Fishkill or South Ward and their heirs and assigns forever' was purchased from Johannis Terboss—and this was the first church built in Rombout Precinct "

Probably the fullest description extant of the appearance of both the present church and the

one which preceded it is given by Henry Du
Bois Bailey, Esq., in his historical sketch of Fishkill Village. Mr. Bailey says : " The old church
was built of stone in the year 1731. In shape
it was quadrangular and the roof came up from
all sides to the centre. From the apex of the
roof ascended the cupola, in that the bell was
suspended, and surmounting the cupola was
the bird which veered with the wind and told
from what quarter of the compass it came. In
front of the church was large oak tree whose
limbs extended across the street. The church
was used as a prison during the Revolution and
the celebrated spy Enoch Crosby who figured
in Cooper's writings as Harvey Birch was con-
fined there, and tradition says that he made his
escape on one dark stormy night by leaping from
an upper window to a limb of this tree. The tree
was taken down when the present edifice was
erected, but the exact year of rebuilding is not
definitely known, the records of that portion of
the church's history being lost, but it must have
been only a few years after the Revolution.
When the present edifice was built the church
was enlarged and extended further west on
Main Street, covering Madame Brett's family
burying plot, and she and some of her children

and grandchildren repose under the present church. On the rebuilding, a tower and steeple were added and the height of the spire is 120 feet. The walls are three feet thick and thirty feet in height. The timbers placed upon the walls to support the roof and tower are of oak and of enormous size, and the building appears as durable now as when first finished. The architect's name was Barnes, and every timber, load of stone, lime and sand was carted to the ground by the congregation gratuitously. There has been no alteration in the exterior of the church except a recess in the rear wall. The interior has been remodeled several times. Originally the galleries were supported from the ceilings with iron rods fastened to the timbers above the arch. Then there were no columns in the church to distract the view and the pulpit and side pews were elevated six inches above the floor. The first alteration was made in 1806, when the iron rods were taken down, the pulpit and side pews lowered, and columns placed underneath the galleries. The second alteration was made in 1820, when the entrance on Main Street was closed, the pews all taken up, new aisles made, pews lowered, and one entrance only, and that in the tower.   The third and last alteration was made in 1854, when the interior was entirely remodeled, with new and modern pews and pulpit, the galleries narrowed and lowered, and a number of pews added to the audience room, and a furnace placed underneath."

The churchyard surrounding the church was used by the members of the congregation as a place of burial at least as early as January, 1737, and probably earlier, and the latest interment appears from the gravestones to have been made in October, 1880, the congregation, since that time, using as a place of sepulchre, the handsome grounds of the Fishkill Rural Cemetery.

December 1, 1882.   E. W. V V.

JOHN ANTHONY,
Born in the City of New York,
1761,
And died March,
1834.

MARY,
Wife of
WILLIAM ANTHONY,
And daughter of
ENOS WRIGHT,
Died June 20, 1836.
Aged 33 years.

HANNAH WRIGHT,
Wife of
WILLIAM ANTHONY,
Died July 14, 1860.
Aged 46 yrs., 8 mos., 6 dys.

ENOS WRIGHT,
Son of
WM. & HANNAH W. ANTHONY,
Born Jan. 1, 1845.
Died Nov. 22, 1864.

MARY WOOLSEY,
Daughter of
WM. & MARY W. ANTHONY,
Born May 31, 1835.
Died Sept. 25, 1869.

IDA,
Daughter of
EDWARD B. and EMILY ALLEN,
Died Aug. 17, 1863.
Aged 8 mos., 12 dys.

WILLIAM H.,
Son of
WILLIAM L. & MARY E. ALLEN,
Died July 31, 1832.
Aged 3 yrs., 3 mos., 11 dys.

NATHAN,
Son of
NATHAN and MARY ASHLEY,
Died Sept. 8, 1821.
Aged 7 yrs., 3 mos., 5 dys.

ADAM ALLGETT,
Died July 10, 1810.
Aged 82 Years.
Having no children
he bequeathed his Estate
to the Reformed Dutch
Church of Hopewell.

FRANK H.,
Son of
Chas. R. and Sarah E. Anderson,
Died Aug. 10, 1861.
Aged 8 yrs., 11 mos., 6 dys.

H. L. S.
The Remains of
MATHEW BRETT, Esqr., .
who departed this life
June 1, 1771.
Aged xxviii Years, x Months, xv Days.
P. M. S.
Within this house my body lies,
My soul arose above the skies,
When time 's no more I 'll rise and live
To taste the joy that Heaven shall give.

In memory of
FRANCES R. BRETT,
who died
Nov. 12, 1813.
Aged 64 years and 2 months.

April 4, 1834.
ANN AUGUSTA,
Daughter of
James and Helen Ann Brett.
Aged 4 yrs., 9 mos.,

CATHERINE,
Daughter of
James and Helen A. Brett,
Died July 26, 1834.
Aged 8 years, 11 mos., 11 dys.

MATILDA,
Daughter of
James and Helen Brett,
Died Sept. 26, 1829.
Aged 8 mo., 14 dys.

Died
June 17, 1846,
LEWIS H. BRETT,
Son of
JOHN W. and SARAH E. BRETT.
A. E. 9 mos., 2 d's.

LEWIS,
Died
Jan. 5, 1850.
A. E. 1 yr., 3 m., 26 dys.

ANNA,
Died
Jan. 5, 1850.
A. E. 1 mo., 2 dys.

Children of JOHN W. and SARAH BRETT.

ROBERT BRETT,
Died May 21, 1831.
Aged 79 years, 5 months,
& 3 days.

SARAH BRETT,
Died Feb. 23, 1844.
Aged 62 years, 4 mos.

ELIZA BRETT,
Wife of
ROBERT BRETT,
Died Oct. 13, 1839,
Aged 84 Years.

In memory of
CATHERINE,
Daughter of ROBERT & HANNAH BRETT,
who departed this life
Oct. 7, 1798.
Aged 4 years, 9 months, & 15 days.

ROBERT ROMBOUT,
Son of
JAMES and HELEN BRETT,
Died April 8, 1848.
Aged 4 years, 8 mos.

EUPHEMIA,
Daughter of
JAMES and HELEN A. BRETT,
Died Jan. 23, 1842.
Aged 5 mos., 20 dys.

PHILLIP A. BOICE,
Died
May 14, 1855.
A. E. 65 yrs., 11 mos., 19 dys.

WILLIAM HENRY,
Son of
ELIAS and MARGARET BREVOORT,
Born Nov. 23, 1802.
Died June 5, 1858.

ALFRED E. BREVOORT,
Died June 2, 1860,
Aged 55 years, 2 mos.

WILLIAM HENRY,
Son of
ELIAS and MARGARET BREVOORT.
The Lord gave
Nov. 23, 1802.
The Lord has taken away
June 5, 1858.
Blessed be the name of the Lord.

ALFRED BREVOORT,
Died June 2, 1860.
Aged 55 years & 2 months.

MARGARET NICHOLS,
Widow of
James A. Bayard,
Died Sept. 26, 1844.
Aged 54 years.

JOHN N. BAILEY,
Born Nov. 11, 1767.
Died Dec. 16, 1846.
Aged 79 years, 1 month, 5 days.

ELIZABETH,
Wife of John N. Bailey,
Born Jan. 7, 1780.
Died July 17, 1865.
Aged 85 yrs., 6 mos., 10 dys.

MARY BAILEY,
Daughter of
JOHN and ELIZABETH BAILEY,
Died Jan. 2, 1846.
Aged 28 yrs., 10 mos., 29 dys.

ELIZABETH,
Daughter of
JOHN N. and ELIZABETH BAILEY,
Died Feb. 4, 1834.
Aged 12 yrs., 10 mos., 15 dys.

GEORGE BOGERT,
Died Jan. 9, 1835.
Aged 77 yrs., 4 mos., 5 dys.

SUSANNA,
Wife of
GEORGE BOGART,
Died July 7, 1833.
Aged 75 yrs., 11 mos., 22 dys.

Hier Leyde Begraaven
het Lichaam van
ABRAHAM BLOOM.
Gestorven
den 3 dag van September, 1757.

FREDERICK BUNNEL,
Died Apr. 10, 1828.
Aged 67 years.

ANN BUNNEL,
Died May 3, 1838.
Aged 70 years.

JOHN BEDFORD,
Died Jan. 11, 1834.
Aged 77 years.

Mrs. ELENOR BEDFORD,
Wife of
John Bedford,
Died Mar. 12, 1838,
in the 65th year of her age.

EDWARD BEDFORD,
Son of
JOHN BEDFORD,
Died Aug. 27, 1817.
Aged 9 yrs. and 27 dys.

ARTHUR,
Son of
ABRAM A. and SARAH JANE BOGARDUS,
Died May 3, 1839.
Aged 3 yrs., 16 dys.

LEWIS H. WHITE,
Son of
ABM. and SARAH J. BOGARDUS.
Died March 29, 1843.
Aged 5 mos., 26 dys.

JULIETTE HOOGLAND,
Dau. of ABM. & SARAH J. BOGARDUS,
Died Dec. 15, 1853.
Aged 10 mos.

CORNELIUS BOGARDUS,
Died July 6, 1811.
Aged 53 yrs., 5 mos., 14 dys.

ELIZABETH ROE,
Wife of
CORNELIUS C. BOGARDUS,
Died July 16, 1807.
Aged 53 yrs., 4 mos., 10 dys.

ELIZABETH BOGARDUS,
Died Sept. 1, 1814.
Aged 17 yrs., 4 mos., 6 dys.

ELIAS BOGARDUS,
Died
Aug. 28, 1853.
Aged 69 yrs. and 12 dys.

ROBERT BOGARDUS,
Died Sept. 28, 1849.
Aged 64 yrs., 1 mo., 28 dys.

HANNAH MONFORT,
Wife of
ELIAS BOGARDUS,
Died Nov. 9, 1839.
Aged 49 yrs. & 15 dys.

MARY BUNCE,
Slept in Jesus
On the 11th of March, 1839.
Aged 69 years.

JAMES H. BRUMFIELD,
Son of
ANDREW D. and MARY BRUMFIELD,
Died in Danbury, Mar. 20, 1826.
Aged 15 yrs., 5 mos., 27 dys.

GILBERT,
Son of
HENRY and ANN BAXTER,
Died
Nov. 30, 1831.
Aged 1 year, 6 mos.

MARY,
Relict of
GIDEON BAXTER.
In her 83d year.

HARRIET BAXTER,
Died Aug. 14, 1864.
Aged 64 years.

GEORGE W. BAXTER,
Died May 10, 1863.
Aged 57 years.

DANIEL BIRDSALL,
Born on Long Island, Oyster Bay.
Died Jan. 6, 1816.
Aged 92 years, 6 days.

MERBY,
Wife of DANIEL BIRDSALL,
Died Feb. 14, 1799,
Aged 68 yrs., 2 mos., 15 dys.

SAMUEL BIRDSALL,
Died June 19, 1811.
Aged 58 yrs., 3 mos., 30 dys.

In memory of
COL. JOHN BRINCKERHOFF,
Who Deptd. this life the 26th day of March, 1785,
in the 83d year of his age.

Ye pious view this humble shrine :
Here lies a friend of God and thine,
In age advanced as you may see
Near to the age of eighty-three ;
In life his closet was his fare,
His house was known a house of prayer ;
At Jesus' feet in humble strains
He rested and the promise claimed ;
In private and in publick life
A friend to peace, a foe to strife.

In memory of
JANNETIE BRINCKERHOFF,
Wife of Coll. JOHN BRINCKERHOFF,
Who departed this life
Nov. 11, 1792.
Æ. 88 Years.

Hier Lydt Het Lighaam
van
JOHANNIS BRINCKERHOFF.
Overleeden De 5th Dagh van Juny, 1757.
oude zynde 29 Jaar. en 9 Maande.

Hier Leyd. Het Lighaam
van
ANTYE BRINCKERHOFF,
Huys vrow van
JOHANNIS BRINCKERHOFF.
Overleeden de 1st Dagh van Juny, 1754.
oude zynde 22 yaren.

Hier Lydt Het Lighaam
van
DIENA BRINCKERHOFF,
Doghter van JAN. BRINCKERHOFF.
Zynde In de Heere Gerust
De 24 Augustus, 1752, oude Zynde
16 Jaaren.

Hier Lydt Het Lighaam
van
BARBERAETTE BRINCKERHOFF,
Doghter van JAN. BRINCKERHOFF.
Zynde In de Heere Gerust
Den 4 Dagh May, 1752.
Oude Zynde 17 Jaaren 22 Dagen.

Hier Lydt Het Lighaam
van
DIRCK BRINCKERHOFF,
Zoon van
JAN. BRINCKERHOFF.
Zynde In de Heere Gerust
de 16 April, 1764, oudt Zynde
25 Jaar.

Anno 1767 : den 23d October.
In de Heere Gerust
GEERTJE BRINCKERHOFF,
Huys vrow van
DIRCK BRINCKERHOFF.
Oudt Zynde 37 Jaaren.

BENJAMIN V. D. L, BRINCKERHOFF,
Dec. 26, 1820.
Aged 26 years, 2 mos.

In memory of
MARIA BRINCKERHOFF,
Wife of
Wm. B. Hutchins,
who died
April 3, 1843.
A. E. 62 yrs., 5 mos., & 28 days.

In memory of
GEORGE G. BRINCKERHOFF,
who departed this life
April 26, 1812,
in the 70th year of his age.

In memory of
GEORGE BRINCKERHOFF,
who died
June 14, 1834.
Aged 33 yrs., 3 mos., & 15 dys.

In memory of
GERTRUDE,
daughter of
DERICK and SARAH BRINCKERHOFF,
who died Feb. 14, 1822.
A. E. 7 years, 11 mos., & 10 days.

GERTRUDE,
Daughter of
JACOB and DIANA BRINCKERHOFF,
Died
Dec. 27, 1864.
A. E. 89 yrs., 2 mos., & 8 dys.

HANNAH,
Daughter of
JACOB and DIANA BRINCKERHOFF,
Died
Feb. 21, 1876.
A. E. 87 yrs., 7 mos., & 22 dys.

In memory of
LETTY BRINCKERHOFF,
daughter of
JACOB BRINCKERHOFF,
who died
Jan. 24, 1846.
A. E. 68 yrs., 9 mos., 18 dys.

In memory of
JACOB BRINCKERHOFF;
Died
August 5, 1818.
Aged 64.

Hier Lydt Het Lighaam van
FEMMETJE, Geboren, REMSEN,
Huys vrow van
ABRAHAM BRINCKERHOFF
naar Zyn overleeden Weeder gertrout
met ABRAM BLOOM.
Geboren den 25 Oct., 1703 &
Gestorven den 6 Feb., 1771.
Oude Zynde 67 Jaaren, 6 maanden.

The Grave of
ALLETTA
Daughter of
Tunis and Catherine
Brinckerhoff.
Born
Oct. 3, 1793.
Died
Dec. 7, 1871.

The Grave of
ELIZABETH,
Daughter of
Tunis and Catherine
Brinckerhoff.
Born
Jan. 23, 1782.
Died
Feb. 28, 1861.

MATILDA JANE,
Daughter of
Henry and Mary Brinckerhoff,
Died Dec. 9, 1843.
Aged 3 years, 8 months.

In memory of
ARCHIBALD CURRIE, Esqr.,
late merchant of New York,
who died
Apr. 25, 1814.
Aged 76 years
& 6 months.

In memory of
CATHERINE CURRIE,
wife of
ARCHIBALD CURRIE, Esqr.,
who died
May 22, 1817,
in the 74th
year of her age.

In memory of
CATHERINE, daughter of
ARCHIBALD and
CATHERINE CURRIE,
who died
Aug. 30, 1841.
Aged 61 yrs. & 15 days.

In memory of
MARGARET, daughter of
Archibald and Catherine
Currie,
who died Jan. 12, 1852,
In the 68th year of her
age.

CORNELIUS CARMEN,
Died Sept. 23, 1860.
Aged 82 years, 2 months.

MARY,
Wife of
Cornelius Carmen,
Died Jan. 1, 1854.
Aged 50 yrs., 4 mos., 7 days.

SARAH,
Daughter of
Benjamin & J. Conover,
· Died Feb. 18, 1862.
Aged 23 years, 10 mos.

CATHERINE CORCELUS,
Wife of
BENJAMIN LUCAM,
Died Oct. 12, 1800.
Aged 54 Years.

CYNTHIA,
wife of
HENRY CHURCHILL,
who died
Mar. 20, 1816.
Aged 49 years.

ISAAC,
Son of
HENRY and CYNTHIA CHURCHILL,
Died Sept. 14, 1811,
Aged 4 years, 4 mos., 28 days.

AMANDA CORBIN,
Died Feb. 5, 1841.
Aged 17 yrs., 10 mos., 5 dys.

THOS. CORBIN,
Died April 22, 1834.
Aged 39 yrs., 3 mos., 24 days.

CORNELIUS COOPER,
Died April 9, 1824.
Aged 88 yrs., 3 mos., 19 dys.

ELIZABETH,
Wife of
CORNELIUS COOPER,
Born July 1, 1750.
Died Mar. 19, 1798.

JOHN COOPER,
Died Dec. 31, 1811.
Aged 53 yrs., 7 mos., 17 dys.

JANE,
relict of
JOHN COOPER,
Died July 10, 1820.
Aged 57 yrs., 2 mos., 20 dys.

BENJAMIN COOPER,
Died Feb. 10, 1859.
Aged 49 yrs., 7 mos., 20 dys.

ELIZABETH,
wife of
BENJAMIN COOPER,
and daughter of
JOHN and JANE COOPER,
Died Dec. 28, 1815.
Aged 20 yrs., 10 mos., 29 dys.

JACOB COOPER,
Born April 11, 1763.
Died Sept. 5, 1844.

ANN TER BOSS,
Wife of
JACOB COOPER,
Died Aug. 18, 1834.
Aged 69 yrs., 2 dys.

MARTHA COOPER,
Wife of
JOHN O. COOPER,
Died Sept. 18, 1778.
Aged 20 yrs., 8 mos., 26 dys.

JANE COOPER,
Died Dec. 27, 1873.
Aged 75 yrs., 5 mos., 7 dys.

RANCHE COOPER,
Died Jan. 25, 1831.
Aged 82 years.

ANASTATIA,
wife of
DAVID DAVIS,
and daughter of
BARTOW and ANNE WHITE,
Born
Mar. 22, 1817.
Died
Oct. 1, 1871.

ELIZABETH,

Wife of

GEORGE V. R. DAVIS,

Died

Oct. 27, 1857.

A. E. 32 yrs., 9 mos., 7 dys.

ABRAHAM DURYEE

departed this life

May 30, 1802.

Aged 60 Years.

ANNA SCHENCK,

Wife of

ABRAHAM DURYEE,

Born the 26th of April, 1723, O. S.,

and departed this life

Aug. the 1st, 1803, N. S.

Aged 80 Years, 2 months, and 26 days.

Here Lyes the Body of

ABRAHAM DURYEE,

Born November 19, 1737,

and departed this life

April 12, 1764,

In the 27th Year of his Age.

Hier Leydt Begraven Het Lichaam
van
STEEVEN DURYEE,
Overleeden den 20ste dag van December
in t' Jaar Onses Heere, 1776.
Oudt Zynde 32 Jaar., 5 Maanden
en 16 Dagen.

Hier Leydt Begraven
ABRAHAM DURYEE,
Gestorven . . . Jaar 1720, den 6 dag
van April. En Overleeden
den 7 dag van September,
1785.

In memory of
WILLIAM DOBBS,
who departed this life
Sept. 13, 1781.
Aged 65 years.

In memory of
JOSEPH DOBBS,
Son of
WILLIAM DOBBS,
who departed this life
May 19, 1790.
Aged 39 years, 4 months, & 3 days.

CAPTN. PETER DUBOIS
departed this life
March 6, 1781.
Aged 83 years and 9 months.

HANNAH,
wife of
PETER DUBOIS,
departed this life
March 1, 1813.
Aged 69 years, 10 months, and 26 days.

SAMUEL DUBOIS,
son of
PETER P. and HANNAH DUBOIS,
departed this life
December 28, 1792.
Aged 7 years and 7 months.

In memory of
PETER P. DUBOIS,
who departed this life
Aug. 14, 1814.
Aged 74 years, 8 months,
and 26 days.

FREELOVE DUBOIS,
daughter of
JOHN & RACHEL DUBOIS,
Died Aug. 22, 1818.
Aged 21 years, 11 months,
& 10 days.

MARIA DUBOIS,
daughter of
JOHN & RACHEL DUBOIS,
Died Aug. 9, 1816.
Aged 23 years, 6 months,
& 20 days.

In memory of
JOHN DUBOIS,
who died
Nov. 14, 1869.
A. E. 99 yrs., 8 mos., 13 dys.

Sacred to the memory of
RACHEL,
wife of
JOHN DUBOIS,
who departed this life
March 23, 1851.
A. E. 79 years & 6 d's.

GARRETT DUBOIS,
Died Aug. 10, 1802.
Aged 32 yrs., 10 mos., 7 days.

HANNAH,
wife of GARRETT DUBOIS,
Died June 10, 1854.
Aged 75 yrs., 6 mos., 4 days.

ABRAHAM DUBOIS,
Died May 12, 1835.
Aged 59 years, 13 months,
& 21 days.

HENRY,
son of
CHARLES L. & CATHERINE DUBOIS,
Died April 3, 1838.
Aged 3 years, 6 months.

CHRISTIAN DUBOIS,
Died Dec. 17, 1807.
Aged 61 yrs., 6 mos., 4 d'ys.

HANNAH DUBOIS,
Died
Sept. 5, 1868.
A. E. 74 yrs., 4 mos., & 29 dys.

In memory of
Three children of
PETER and HANNAH DUBOIS,
BENJAMIN, ABRAHAM, and ANNE,
who died in the year 1770.

Hier Lyde Het Lighaam
van
PIETER D' BOIS,
Overleeden Den 22 van Januarie,
Anno 1737⅞.   Oude Zynde
63 Jaar.

In memory of
JACOB DUBOIS,
who was born May 1, 1734,
and departed this life
the 24th of Nov., 1795.
Aged 61 years, 6 mo., 24 days.

Here lies the Body
of
JACOB DUBOIS,
who departed this life
June 4, 1783.
Aged 82 Years.

ELIZABETH DUBOIS,
Died
December 12, 1819.
Aged 40 years, 8 mos., 24 dys.

Also
MARTHA CHEESEMAN,
Died
December 12, 1819.
Aged 69 years, 10 mos., 12 d'ys.

Miss ELSIE DUNN,
Died
Oct. 13, 1857.
Aged 58 yrs., 9 mos., 5 d'ys.

MARY,
wife of
JAMES FREAM,
departed this life
July the 20th, 1780.
Aged 29 years.

Also
MARGARET,
Daughter of
JAMES and MARY FREAM,
who died July 21, 1781.
Aged 1 year and 8 days.

HARRIET JANE,
Daughter of
GEORGE H. and ELENOR GORE,
Died Aug. 30, 1841.
Aged 16 days.

LUCY,	DANIEL H.,
Died	Died
Aug. 15, 1848.	Aug. 29, 1849.
Aged 1 yr., 8 mos., 8 dys.	Aged 10 mos.

Children of CHARLES W. and MARY GODFREY.

ELIZA JANE,
Dau. of
WILLIAM and JANE GREY.
Deceased Dec. 15, 1860.
Aged 7 years, 4 mos., 23 dys.

MARY,
daughter of
CHARLES and ELENOR GRIFFIN,
Died Feb. 14, 1834.
Aged 7 mos., 23 dys.

JOHN GRIDLEY,
December 1, 1830.
Aged 81 yrs.

WILLIAM GILDERSLEEVE,
Died Apr. 26, 1848.
Aged 52 years.

MARGARET GRAHAM,
Died Nov. 28, 1845.
Aged 71 yrs., 10 mos., 10 d'ys.

CATHERINE,
daughter of
PETER and ANNA GRAHAM,
Died Ap'l 22, 1822.
Aged 5 mos., 14 days.

MARY,
daughter of
E. VAN WILLIAMS and CATHERINE GRAHAM,
Died Oct. 13, 1803.
Aged 1 year, 6 mos., 6 days.

DUNCAN,
son of
DUNCAN GRAHAM,
Died June 25, 1797.
Aged 20 yrs., 4 mos.

DUNCAN GRAHAM,
Died
Feb. 23, 1835.
Aged 94 yrs., 3 mos., 8 days.

ELIZABETH BATES,
wife of
DUNCAN GRAHAM,
Died March 12, 1804.
Aged 48 yrs., 8 mos.

ANN,
wife of
DUNCAN GRAHAM,
Died Feb. 23, 1853.
Aged 78 years, 18 days.

JOHN,
son of
DUNCAN & ELIZABETH GRAHAM,
Died Oct. 2, 1804.
Aged 5 yrs., 4 mos., 7 days.

MARY,
daughter of
DUNCAN GRAHAM,
Died Aug. 20, 1805.
Aged 26 yrs., 11 mos., 20 days.

PETER GRAHAM,
son of
DUNCAN GRAHAM,
Died June 4, 1822.
Aged 52 years, 5 mos.

ANNA,
wife of
PETER GRAHAM,
and daughter of
SIMON & ELIZABETH DEGRAEFF,
Died June 15, 1856.
Aged 77 yrs., 7 mos., 19 days.

In memory of
JAMES GIVEN,
who was born in Cullybackey,
Ireland,
April 12, 1777.
Came to America in 1798,
and after a residence in this
Village of more than sixty years,
Died Nov. 5, 1862,
In the 86th year of his age.

In memory of
SUSAN VAN WYCK,
wife of
JAMES GIVEN,
who died
July 8, 1862,
In the 78 Year
of her Age.

In memory of
VAN WYCK GIVEN,
who was born in
Fishkill,
Aug. 15, 1818,
and died in the Retreat
for the Insane
at
Brattleborough, Vt.,
Dec. 5, 1846.
A. E. 28 years.

ELIZABETH SHEAR,
Daughter of
RUDOLPHUS HASBROOK,
Died Nov. 11, 1841.
Aged 88 yrs., 11 mos.,
& 7 days.

JACOB HASBROOK,
Died
May 7, 1849,
in his 69th year.

CORNELIUS C.,
son of
CORNELIUS & SARAH HAYNES,
Died Aug. 27, 1830.
Aged 3 years, 3 mos., 18 days.

JANE HAYNES,
Departed this life
Dec. 27, 1831.
Aged 42 years, 2 months.

Here lyeth the Remains of
PATRICK HEANEY,
native of Irishtown,
County Antrim, Ireland,
who died
May 5, 1853.
A. E. 42 Years.
This Stone is erected by his disconsolate widow.

SARAH,
wife of
JOHN B. HAUK,
Died Oct. 23, 1794.
Aged 56 yrs., 2 mos., 10 d'ys.

PHEBE,
widow of
JAMES HUMPHREY,
Died Jan. 8, 1840.
In the 82d year of her age.

JOSEPH J. JACKSON,
Born Oct. 24, 1783.
Died Aug. 2, 1863.

ANN JANE,
wife of
JOSEPH J. JACKSON,
Died Feb. 2, 1832.
Aged 44 yrs., 6 mos., 6 dys.

THEODORE WILSON,
son of
JOSEPH J. and SARAH JACKSON,
Died June 8, 1841.
Aged 3 yrs., 10 mos., 28 d'ys.

EDWARD M. JACKSON,
Died July 14, 1832.
Aged 7 years, 5 mos., 20 days.

FLORINDA S. JOHNSON,
Died
Aug. 7, 1854.
Aged 24 years, 3 mos., 22 days.

Anno 1771, Den 22d September,
In De Heere Gerust
CATHERINE LAWRENCE,
Huys vrow van
LAWRENCE LAWRENCE.
Oudt Zynde 42 Jaaren,
9 maanden, en 4 dagen.

In memory of
MAGDELENE,
wife of
Mr. ABM. LYNSEN of N. York,
who departed this life
Sept. 20, 1783.
Aged 40 years.

Here Lyes the Body of
SILAS LOCKWOOD,
Borne Sept. 3, 1743.
Died Sept. 10, 1768.
Aged 25 years, 7 days.

MAHALA,
wife of
JESSE B. LADUE,
Died Dec. 27, 1843.
Aged 29 yrs., 10 mos., 27 d'ys.

ISABELLA,
wife of
ABRAHAM LIDDLE,
Daughter of
ROBERT & JANE KAY,
Died Mar. 4, 1849.
Aged 21 yrs., 10 mos.

JAMES,
son of
ABRAHAM & ISABELLA LIDDLE,
Died Jan. 26, 1849.
Aged 5 mos., 4 dys.

MATILDA,
wife of
NATHAN LANE,
Died Feb. 4, 1840.
Aged 20 yrs., 10 mos., 6 d'ys.

ADRIAN MONFORT,
Died Feb. 6, 1849.
Aged 94 Years.

ALLETTA WALDRON,
wife of
ADRIAN MONFORT,
Died July 29, 1802.
Aged 38 yrs., 7 months.

MATILDA MONFORT,
Died Sept. 28, 1833.
Aged 26 years & 2 months.

SARAH MILLS,
Died June 15, 1851.
Aged 80 yrs., 4 mos., 3 dys.

WILLIAM McNEAL,
Died Jan. 15, 1834.
Aged 56 years.

MARY,
relict of
WILLIAM McNEAL,
Died Feb. 8, 1857.

ESTHER,
daughter of
STEPHEN & REBECCA E. MORRIS,
Died Aug. 7, 1831.
Aged 8 years, 6 mos., 7 days.

STEPHEN MORRIS,
Died Apr. 19, 1837.
Aged 36 years, 6 mos.,
3 days.

POLLY,
wife of
SHELDON MARTIN,
Died March 15, 1827.
Aged 40 yrs. & 15 dys.

SHELDON W.,
son of
SHELDON and POLLY MARTIN,
Died Aug. 29, 1825.
Aged 11 weeks & 6 days.

Hier Leyde het Lighaam
van
CATRINA RAPALJE,
Huys vrow van Dom' Benj. Meenema,
in de Heere Ontslaapen
Den 17th January, 1759.
Oude Synde 28 Jaar
en 6 maanden.

Hier Leyde het Lighaam
van De Feiwaarde Heer
BENJAMIN MEENEMA,
in hyn Leenens Teje predikant van de
Viskels & Poughkeepsie, in de
Heere Ontslaapen den 9 September, 1761.
Oude Synde 56 Jaar.

SAMUEL,
Died Mar. 27, 1858.
Aged 10 yrs., 7 mos.
Son of Levi & Mary Niven.

JOSEPHUS,
son of
GILBERT & ABIGAIL NIVEN,
Died Sept. 14, 1855.
A. E. 3 mos. & 14 days.

GEORGE R.,
son of
GILBERT & ABIGAIL NIVEN,
Died April 9, 1854.
A. E. 1 yr., 11 mos., 27 days.

EUGENE,
son of
GILBERT & ABIGAIL NIVEN,
Died Sept. 14, 1853.
A. E. 5 mos., 24 days.

ROSINA,
daughter of
GILBERT & ABIGAIL NIVEN,
Died Dec. 25, 1850.
A. E. 2 mos., 18 days.

WILLIAM B. OWEN,
son of
THOMAS OWEN,
Died
May 3, 1843.
Aged 37 yrs., 10 m., 3 d'ys.

EMMA,
daughter of
MERRITT & SARAH OWEN,
Died May 28, 1843.
Aged 11 days.

PHEBE,
wife of
MERRITT OWEN,
Died
Feb. 13, 1837.
Aged 38 yrs., 1 mo.,
13 days.

ALBERT,
infant son of
MERRITT & SARAH A. OWEN,
Died Dec. 4, 1850.   A. E. 5 mos.

GEORGE B.,
Son of
MERRITT & SARAH OWEN,
Died Aug. 27, 1852. .
Aged 8 years.

ELIZABETH PEPPER,
Died Mar. 24, 1853.
Aged 51 Years, 9 m., 22 d'ys.

OBEDIAH PEPPER,
Died June 16, 1841.
Aged 24 Years, 12 mos., 18 d'ys.

CORNELIUS PEPPER,
Born April 28, 1819.
Died May 8, 1854.

ELIJAH PEPPER,
Died July 9, 1839.
Aged 59 Y'rs., 2 mos., 10 d'ys.

MARY,
wife of
ELIJAH PEPPER,
Died September 8, 1831.
Aged 77 Years, 10 months.

ELIAS PEPPER,
Died
Dec. 16, 1838.   A. E. 26 yrs.

WILLIAM PEPPER,
Died
April 28, 1863.
Aged 59 Years,
1 month, 17 days.

ISAAC PEPPER,
Died March 11, 1834
Aged
28 Years.

ELIJAH PEPPER,
Died April 29, 1870.
Aged 21 yrs., 1 mo.

THOMAS D. PEPPER,
Died Feb. 25, 1870.
Aged 26 yrs., 1 mo., 10 days.

CHARLOTTE,
wife of
CORNELIUS PEPPER,
Born Oct. 7, 1821.
Died Aug. 15, 1849.

ELENOR PUDNEY,
Died Sept. 12, 1831.
Aged 91 years, 8 mos., 29 d'ys.

ANNE,
daughter of
———. R. PARMELEE,
Died Dec. 20, 1827.
Aged 1 year, 2 months.

BENJAMIN PECK,
son of
STEPHEN PECK
of New York,
Died June 29, 1835.
Aged 29 years.

HANNAH,
daughter of
DANIEL S. & CYNTHIA PHILLIPS,
Died June 8, 1834.
Aged 9 years, 4 mos.

HENRY H. PHILLIPS,
Died Nov. 22, 1830.
Aged 77 yrs., 9 mos., 17 days.

SARAH,
wife of
HENRY H. PHILLIPS,
Died Oct. 25, 1838.
Aged 74 yrs., 11 mos., 26 days.

JOHN R. PHILLIPS,
Died Dec. 2, 1832.
Aged 76 years.

ELIZABETH CANNIFF,
wife of
JOHN R. PHILLIPS,
Died Nov. 22, 1808.
Aged 53 yrs., 7 mos., 18 dys.

JONIS,
son of
JOHN R. PHILLIPS,
Died Oct. 15, 1812.
Aged 13 yrs., 7 mos., 17 days.

DANIEL J. PHILLIPS,
Died Mar. 28, 1856.
Aged 57 yrs., 2 days.

DANIEL PHILLIPS,
Died Aug. 2, 1848.
Aged 63 yrs., 10 mo., 26 dys.

REBECCA,
wife of
DANIEL PHILLIPS,
Died Nov. 23, 1811.
Aged 22 yrs., 15 days.

CYNTHIA PHILLIPS,
Died Dec. 3, 1851.
Aged 80 yrs., 9 d'ys.

HANNAH,
dau' of
DANIEL & CYNTHIA PHILLIPS,
Died May 8, 1812.   Aged 2 yrs., 6 mos.

CAROLINE,
dau' of
DANIEL & CYNTHIA PHILLIPS,
Died July 29, 1820. Aged 1 yr., 4 mos., 5 d'ys.

DEBORAH,
Daughter of
HENRY & SARAH PHILLIPS,
Born April 3, 1786.
Died Oct. 17, 1861.

ABRAHAM PHILLIPS,
Died May 22, 1838.
Aged 50 yrs., 3 mos., 15 dys.

JEROME PHILLIPS,
Died June 24, 1858.
Aged 33 yrs., 4 mos., 8 d'ys.

MARY ELIZABETH,
wife of
JEROME PHILLIPS,
Died April 25, 1849.
Aged 19 yrs., 7 mos., 21 d'ys.

MARY J. PHILLIPS,
Born Oct. 12, 1829.
Died Oct. 7, 1853.

The Grave of
SARAH POLLOCK,
who died
Oct. 10, 1874,
In the 93d year
of her age.

" In the world to come life everlasting."

LUKE xviii: 30.

Little
MELISSA,
Daughter of
GEORGE and ELIZABETH PEARSALL,
Died Mar. 8, 1860.
AE. 1 yr., 10 mos., 18 dys.

To perpetuate the remembrance
of
an amiable and beloved son,
a kind and affectionate brother,
a faithful friend,
and a
sincere and exemplary Christian,
This Cenotaph
is erected by
the bereaved and afflicted family
of
WILLIAM EDWARD RAPALJE,
who died at sea
on his return from Europe,
on the 2d day of June,
1833,
in the 31st year of his age.
His body
was solemnly committed
to the deep.

In memory of
JOHN AUGUSTUS,
son of
RICHARD and JANE RAPALJE,
who died Oct. 6, 1806.
Aged 1 day.

In memory of
ELIZA VAN WYCK,
daughter of RICHARD
& LETTY RAPALJE,
who departed this life
Jan. 17, 1801.
Aged 10 months & 11 days.

In memory of
ELIZABETH RAPALJE,
daughter of
RICHARD RAPALJE,
deceased 17th September, 1796.
Aged 5 months & 23 days.

In memory of
JOHN VAN WYCK,
son of RICHARD & LETTY
RAPALJE,
who departed this life
Sept. 15, 1798,
Aged 26 days.

Sacred to the memory of
LETTY,
wife of Major RICHARD RAPALJE,
and daughter of ISAAC VAN WYCK, Esqr.,
who departed this life Septr.
11, 1800.
Aged 24 years, 9 months & 11 days.

Sacred to the memory of
JANE,
wife of Major RICHARD RAPALJE,
and daughter of
ISAAC VAN WYCK, Esqr.,
who departed this life
Nov. 23, 1806.
Aged 24 years, 8 months & 9 days.

Still lives the memory of departed worth
The tear is holy that bedews its sod
Although the fading form is laid in Earth
The living mind 's ascended to its God.

In memory of
ISAAC VAN WYCK,
son of
RICHARD & JANE RAPALJE,
Deceased Dec. 7, 1809.
Aged 5 years & 30 days.

Sacred to the memory of
ISAAC VAN WICK RAPALJE,
son of Richard and
Ann Rapalje.
He died 31st of July, 1824,
in the 12th year of his age.

*" Man cometh forth like a flower
and is cut down."*

Sacred to the memory of
JANE ANN RAPALJE,
daughter of Richard
and Ann Rapalje.
She died 4th July, 1825,
in the 14th year of her age.

*From adverse blasts and lowering storms
Her favored soul he bore
And with yon bright angelic forms
She lives to die no more.*

Glory to God alone.
Sacred to the memory of
RICHARD RAPALJE.

He was born on Long Island 30th of August,
1764. Removed to Fishkill during our Revo-
lutionary struggle when but a youth, where by
the most unremitting industry and application
to business he soon rose to independence, re-
spectability and usefulness attained by few.
Active in publick, interesting in social, and
amiable in private life, he lived to bless his day
and generation, and fell asleep the 2d of September, 1825.

Aged 61 years and 2 days.

The Grave of
RICHARD RAPALJE,
son of
RICHARD and ANN RAPALJE.
Exemplary in every relation of life
and endeared by his many virtues
to all who knew him
he
while the prospect of many years
of continued usefulness
was bright
yielded his spirit to God
on the 26th of December, 1846,
in the 32d year of his age.

" Be ye also ready for in such an hour
as ye think not the son of man
cometh."
MATH xxiv : 44.

Sacred to the memory
of
ARCHIBALD CURRIE RAPALJE,
son of
RICHARD and ANN RAPALJE,
who died July 28, 1831.
Aged 14 years,
6 months and 12 days.

Though death the strongest tie did sever
And vailed each earthly joy in gloom
Must all our hopes, sweet youth, forever
Be laid with thee in this dark tomb
No ! there is left one beam of light
One cheering hope to us is given
The sting of death can never blight
The hope of meeting thee in Heaven.

The Grave of
ANN,
wife of
RICHARD RAPALJE,
and daughter of
ARCHIBALD and CATHERINE
CURRIE.
Born
September 13, 1777.
Died
January 31, 1860.

Whom have I in Heaven but thee?
and there is none upon the Earth
that I desire besides thee.
My flesh and my heart faileth,
but God is the strength of my heart,
and my portion forever.

The Grave of
CATHERINE ELIZABETH,
wife of
ISAAC E. COTHEAL,
and daughter of
RICHARD and ANN
RAPALJE.
Born
July 8, 1819.
Died
Jan. 8, 1864.

Sacred to the
memory of
MARY,
wife of
Abraham B. Rapalje, Esqr.,
who departed this life
Nov. 2, 1808.
Aged 44 years, 5 months
& 6 days.
A tender mother and a virtuous wife,
Prudent in all the needful cares of life.

In memory of
ABRAHAM B. RAPALJE, Esqr.,
who died
Jan. 12, 1818.
Aged 57 years
8 months
& 26 days.

The Grave of
STEPHEN RAPALJE,
Surgeon in
The United States Navy,
who died at sea
on board the
U. S. Frigate Wabash
Sept. 11, 1856.
Aged 68 years.

Erected to the memory of
JOHN A. RAPALJE,
who died Nov. 3, 1815.
Aged 30 years.
and 8 months.

PHEBE ELIZA,
wife of
SAMUEL BOWNE,
and daughter of
ABRAHAM B. RAPALJE,
Born
Oct 31, 1796.
Died
Oct. 10, 1880.
Joy cometh in the morning.

SAMUEL BOWNE,
Born
June 23, 1795.
Died
July 25, 1848.
For so he giveth his beloved sleep.

STEPHEN RAPALJE,
son of
SAMUEL & PHEBE ELIZA
BOWNE,
Born
July 11, 1827.
Died
May 9, 1880.
Blessed are the pure in heart.

J. Sacred R
to the memory of
JERONIMUS E. RAPALJE,
who died
Jan. 3, 1840,
in the 35th year
of his age.

ADELAIDE,
Daughter of
SYLVANUS and SUSAN RAPALJE,
Born Aug. 7, 1824.
Died May 28, 1825.
Aged 9 mos., 21 days.

JOHN M. ROSEKRANS,
Born May 28, 1779.
Died Dec. 26, 1843.

JOHN ROSEKRANS,
Died Dec. 31, 1831.
Aged 69 yrs., 2 d'ys.

MARY HICKS,
wife of
JOHN ROSEKRANS,
Died Jan. 13, 1849.
Aged 82 years, 4 mos.,
18 days.

ANN MARIA,
daughter of
JOHN & MARY ROSEKRANS,
Died Oct. 29, 1820.
Aged 23 yrs., 4 mos., 20 d'ys.

MARY,
daughter of
JAMES & SARAH ANN ROSEKRANS,
Died May 4, 1823.
Aged 3 yrs., 4 mos., 20 d'ys.

SARAH ANN,
daughter of
LEMUEL and MARY ANN REED,
Died Sept. 19, 1816.
Aged 1 year & 5 months.

EDWARD REMSEN,
Born Feb. 27, 1800.
Died Nov. 24, 1878.

JOHN REMSEN,
Died Oct. 8, 1809.
Aged 26 yrs., 1 mo., 22 d'ys.

CHARLOTTE M.,
wife of
JOHN RANOUS,
Died Jan 31, 1856.
Aged — yrs., 5 mos., 22 dys.

ZEBULON SOUTHARD,
Died Oct. 20, 1854.
Aged 77 yrs., 3 mos., 9 d'ys.

CATHERINE,
wife of
ZEBULON SOUTHARD,
Died May 31, 1854.
Aged 76 yrs., 7 mos., 16 days.

ADELINE,
daughter of
ZEBULON & CATHERINE SOUTHARD,
Died May 29, 1832.
Aged 10 yrs., 2 mos., 15 d'ys.

MARY IDA,
daughter of
JOHN H. & CAROLINE SOUTHARD,
Died Mar. 8, 1859.
Aged 12 yrs., 1 mo., 15 days.

HARVEY R.,
son of
JOHN H. & CAROLINE SOUTHARD,
Died May 14, 1859.
Aged 2 yrs., 4 mos., 25 dys.

ELIZABETH,
wife of
JOHN D. SMITH,
Died Jan. 20, 1844.
Aged 51 years, 11 mos., 28 days.

CHARLES EDGAR,
son of JOHN D. & ELIZABETH SMITH,
Died Sept. 2, 1839.
Aged 3 years, 11 mos., 10 days.

MARY SMITH,
Died Apr. 21, 1842.
In the 86th year of her age.

HANNAH COOPER,
wife of
STEPHEN SMITH,
Died Sept. 4, 1799.
Aged 36 yrs., 7 mos., 10 dys.

ABRAHAM SMITH,
Born in the City of New York
the 9th day of Feb., 1732.
Died Sept. 1, 1817.
Aged 85 years.

MARY,
wife of
ABRAHAM SMITH,
Died Feb. 6, 1808.
Aged 67 years.

ADELIA,
wife of
HENRY SLAUSON,
Died Sept. 11, 1851.
Aged 28 yrs., 8 mos., 15 dys.

HETTY ANN,
wife of
JOSEPH SLAUSON,
Died Mar. 26, 1857.
Aged 31 yrs., 2 mos., 3 d'ys.

GEORGE S.,
son of
Wm. H. & Jamanda Strang,
Died Sept. 14, 1845.
Aged 4 weeks.

HARRIET,
daughter of
David and Catherine Sturges,
who dep'd this life
December 10, 1795.
Aged 3 years, 4 months, & 3 days.

In memory of
CORNELIUS SEBRING,
of
New York,
who departed this life
Aug. the 6th, 1778.
Aged 62 Years
and 6 months.

In memory of
SARAH SEBRING,
wife of
Cornelius Sebring,
who departed this life
Aug. 16, 1792.
Aged 52 Years
and 6 months.

Sacred to the memory of
ISAAC SEBRING,
son of
CORNELIUS & ALETHEA SEBRING,
who died
May 1, A.D. 1841.
Aged 84 yrs., 4 mos.
& 10 days.

In memory of
MARGARET CURRIE,
daughter of
CORNELIUS & ALTHEA SEBRING,
who died
Nov. 9, 1842.
Aged 92 Years, 10 months, & 4 days.

SARAH LETITIA,
Born Feb. 18, 1858.
Died Nov. 28, 1858.

NEWELL WYETH,
Born Jan. 27, 1860.
Died Aug. 14, 1861.
Children of NICHOLAS H. & PHEBE C. STRIPPEL.

NICHOLAS STRIPPEL,
Born in Germany
Aug. 23, 1782,
Died at Fishkill
April 22, 1847.
Aged 64 yrs., 8 mos.

CATHERINE O. SWARTWOUT,
Born
Jan. 30, 1798.
Died
Nov. 18, 1873.

THOMAS OSBORN,
Born
July 27, 1764.
Died
Oct. 13, 1845.

CATHERINE OSBORN,
Born
Dec. 25, 1766.
Died
Apr. 17, 1837.

Hier Lydt Het Lighaam
van
JACOBUS SWARTWOUT,
Zynde In de Heere Gerust
Den 3 Dagh van April, 1749.
Oude Zynde 57 Jaar., 1 maande
en 20 Dagen.

CORNELIUS,
son of
SIMON and RUTH SWARTWOUT,
Died Sept. 8, 1831.
Aged 22 yrs., 4 mos.

MARY SWART,
wife of
EVERT WYNKOOP SWART,
Born Nov. 1, 1729.   Died Mar. 7, 1792.
Aged 62 yrs., 3 mos., 25 dys.

ISAAC SCHOFIELD,
Died Oct. 27, 1827,
In the 31st year of his age.

In memory of
JEROME SCHOFIELD,
who died
Nov. 1, 1850.
AE. 70 Years,
3 mos.

In memory of
ELIZABETH,
wife of
JEROME SCHOFIELD,
who died
April 8, 1850.
AE. 67 Yrs., 1 mo., 5 dys.

DERRICK
son of
JACOB I. & DINAH SCOFIELD,
who died
Dec. 2, 1855.
A.E. 25 yrs., 8 mos. & 56 dys.

In memory of
MARIA ELIZABETH,
wife of
JOHN R. MYER,
& daughter of
JEROME and ELIZABETH SCOFIELD,
who died
June 26, 1848.
A.E. 35 yrs. & 3 mos.

DINAH,
daughter of
JEROME and ELIZABETH SCOFIELD,
who died
March 17, 1811.
Aged 17 days.

In memory of
JACOB I. SCOFIELD,
who died
Jan. 28, 1856.
A.E. 59 yrs., 9 mos., 22 d'ys.

In memory of
DINAH,
wife of
JACOB I. SCOFIELD,
who died
May 14, 1870.
A.E. 77 Y'rs, 5 m., 27 d'ys.

DANIEL TOWNSEND,
Born at Norwich, Long Island,
Aug. 26, 1785.
Died Aug. 17, 1825.

CYNTHIA,
daughter of
DANIEL and ELIZABETH TOWNSEND,
Died Sept., 12, 1816.
Aged 5 mos., 5 d'ys.

GIDEON TOWNSEND, JR.,
Died Apr. 3, 1823.
Aged 32 years.

CAROLINE M.,
Daughter of
Edward & Rachel A. Teller.
Aged 5 yrs., 6 mos., 8 dys.

ADOLPH VANDEWATER,
Born September, 1760.
Died August, 1830.
Aged 70 Years.

WILLIAM,
son of
Jacob & Elizabeth Van Tassel,
Died July 3, 1769.
Aged 3 months.

Here lyes the Body	Here lyes the Body
of IOHN VAN VOORHIS.	of BARBARA VAN DYCK.
Aged 75 Years.	Aged 59 Years.
Deceased Oct. 10,	Deceased Apr. 18,
A° 1757.	A° 1743.

Here lyes the Body of
JACOB VAN VOORHIS,
who Departed this life
the 17th day of January, 1780.
Aged 56 years,
3 months & 3 days.

In memory of
ZACHARIUS VAN VOORHIS,
who departed this life
Jan'y ye 20th, 1784.
Aged 74 Years.

In
memory of
Major WILLIAM ROE VAN VOORHIS.
Died Nov. 2, 1828,
in his 64th year.

In
memory of
RACHEL VAIL,
wife of
William Roe Van Voorhis.
Died June 12, 1845,
In the 78 year of her age.

In
memory of
WILLIAM ROE VAN VOORHIS.
Died July 16, 1833,
in the 24th year of his age.

JULIA VAN VOORHIS,
wife of
JOHN T. RICH,
Died Mar. 9, 1840.
Aged 28 years.

LOUISE RICH,
daughter of
JULIA & JOHN T. RICH.
Aged 20 mos.

ELIZABETH VAN VOORHIS,
wife of
STEPHEN SCHOUTEN,
Died Aug. 22, 1855.
Aged 77 years.

DANIEL VAN VOORHIS,
Died April 22, 1842.
Aged 61 years, 11 mos., 12 days.

JEROMUS,
son of
DANIEL I. and MARTHA VAN VOORHIS.
Died May 14, 1839.
Aged 1 year, 25 days.

CHRISTIAN VAN VOORHIS,
Born Sept. 11, 1788.
Died April 6, 1853.

SAMUEL VAN VOORHIS.
Died Sept. 28, 1848.
Aged 75 years, 9 mos., 2 days.

SARAH COOPER,
wife of
SAMUEL VAN VOORHIS,
Died Aug. 9, 1859.
Aged 83 years, 7 m's, 16 days.

ELIZABETH,
wife of
JOHN VAN VOORHIS,
and daughter of
JOHN COOK,
Born in New Jersey, Mar. 28, 1798.
Died March 4, 1857.

HENRY,
son of
DANIEL I. VAN VOORHIS,
Died Apr. 11, 1833.
Aged 1 year, 1 mo., 29 dys.

MATTHEW B. VAN VOORHIS,
Died May 19, 1855.
Aged 26 years, 4 mos., 17 days.

JOHN VAN VOORHIS,
Died Dec. 28, 1854.
Aged 21 years, 10 months,
14 days.

ELIZABETH,
daughter of
Zebulon T., & Elizabeth Van Voorhis,
Died Feb. 16, 1832.
Aged 1 year, 2 months, 5 days.

The Grave of
WM. C. VAN VOORHIS,
who was born
Feb. 15, 1822,
and died
March 21, 1857.

Also
In memory of
CORNELIUS VAN VOORHIS,
who was born
August 26, 1816,
and died at the Battle of
Pitsburgh Landing,
Apr. 6, 1862.

Shall not the Judge of all the earth do right?

ANN S.,
wife of
ZACHARIAH VAN VOORHIS,
Died Feb. 9, 1851.
Aged 88 years, 8 mos., 24 days.

ANNA LAWRENCE,
wife of
ZACHARIAH VAN VOORHIS,
Born Aug. 24, 1751.
Died Dec. 10, 1781.

SARAH VAN VOORHIS,
Died April 14, 1860.
Aged 67 years, 27 days.

ABRAHAM Z. VAN VOORHIS,
Died Aug. 19, 1870.
Aged 75 years, 6 mos., 3 days.

HELLENAH VAN VOORHIS,
wife of
CHRISTIAN DUBOIS,
Died Mar. 4, 1826.
Aged 82 years, 10 mos., 4 days.

ELIZABETH VAN VOORHIS,
Born March 8, 1795.
Died Jan. 22, 1875.

ZACHARIAH VAN VOORHIS,
Died July 3, 1811.
Aged 63 years, 4 mos., 13 days.

Died
April 12, 1832,
MARY ANN,
daughter of
HENRY and MARY VAN VOORHIS.
Aged 8 mos. & 22 days.

HANNAH,
daughter of
Samuel L. Van Voorhis & Sarah Cooper,
Died Nov. 25, 1812.
Aged 1 year, 4 mos., 2 days.

JANE ROBINSON,
wife of
Peter Van Voorhis,
Died Nov. 7, 1858.
Aged 60 years, 5 mos., 7 days.

CORNELIUS VAN VOORHIS,
Died Sept. 20, 1838.
Aged 68 years, 4 mos., 8 days.

CATHERINE,
wife of
Cornelius Van Voorhis,
Died June 2, 1814.
Aged 44 years, 4 mos., 18 dys.

ABRAHAM VAN VOORHIS,
Born Sept. 14, 1794.
Died May 21, 1868.
Aged 73 years, 8 mos., 7 days.

ABBEY,
wife of
ABRAHAM VAN VOORHIS,
Died March 17, 1828.
Aged 28 years, 6 mos., 14 days.

HANNAH,
wife of
ABRAHAM VAN VOORHIS,
Died April 5, 1842.
Aged 43 years, 1 m., 13 dys.

MARY ANN,
daughter of
SAMUEL L. VAN VOORHIS & SARAH COOPER,
Born Dec. 19, 1803.   Died June 20, 1844.

AUGUSTUS T.,
son of
JOHN & ELIZABETH VAN VOORHIS,
Died Oct. 5, 1819.
Aged 9 months.

HENRY VAN VOORHIS,
Born Nov. 3, 1801.
Died April 28, 1845.
Aged 43 years, 5 mos., 25 days.

DANIEL I. VAN VOORHIS,
Died Dec. 27, 1850.
Aged 50 years, 21 days.

RICHARD RAPALJE,
son of
DANIEL I. & MARTHA VAN VOORHIS,
Died May 1, 1851.
Aged 10 mos., 17 days.

MARGARET,
wife of
DANIEL VAN VOORHIS,
Died Jan'y 20, 1859.
Aged 71 yrs., 5 m., 9 days.

BARTOW W. VAN VOORHIS,
son of CHRISTIAN & ELIZABETH VAN VOORHIS.

Glory
to God alone.
Sacred to the memory of
The
REVEREND NICHOLAS VAN VRANKEN,
Minister of Jehovah Jesus, and Pastor of the
Dutch Reformed Congregations of Fishkill,
Hopewell, and New Hackensack. This excel-
lent man lived tenderly beloved and died deeply
lamented by the people of his charge. He was
born the 24th of May, 1762, and departed in
peace and rested in hope the 20th of May, 1804.
Aged 41 Years, 11 months & 19 Days.

In memory of
RUTHY COMSTOCK,
the first wife of
The Rev. Nicholas Van Vranken.
She was born the 31st of December, 1763,
and died the 16th of August, 1800.
Aged 36 years, 4 mos.
and 14 days.

ALBERT,
son of
Cornelius C. & Letitia Van Wyck,
Born Feb. 25, 1805.
Died Nov. 23, 1806.

In memory of
WILLIAM W. VAN WYCK,
who died
Aug. 27, 1840.
Aged 63 Years.

HARRIET C. STAGG,
wife of
Wm. C. Van Wyck,
Died at Sudley, Fairfax Co., Va.,
Aug. 14, 1825.
A. E. 42 Years.

In memory of
SARAH,
daughter of
William & Sarah Van Wyck.
Died
Nov. 20, 1854.
Aged 80 Years.

In memory of
AMELIA MATILDA,
wife of
Isaac I. Van Wyck,
& daughter of Joseph Jackson,
who died
Sept. 11, 1848.
A. E. 52 yrs., 1 mo., 20 d'ys.

In memory of
FULTON,
son of
WILLIAM & HARRIET VAN WYCK,
who died
Oct. 27, 1818.
Aged 8 months.

In memory of
MARIA,
Daughter of
ISAAC & ELIZABETH VAN WYCK,
who departed this life
October the 7th, 1805.
Aged 15 years, 11 months and 7 days.

In memory of
ELIZABETH,
daughter of
ISAAC VAN WYCK,
who died
Jan. 31, 1845,
in the 66th year of her age.

In memory of
CORNELIUS I. VAN WYCK, Esq'r,
son of
Isaac Van Wyck, Esq'r,
who departed this life
Feb'y 17, 1804.
Aged 19 Years, 4 months & 14 Days.

In memory of
ISAAC I.,
son of
Isaac Van Wyck,
who died
Mar. 22, 1862.
A. E. 69 Yrs., 5 mos., 20 days.

In memory of
CHARLES YOUNG VAN WYCK,
who died
Feb'y 10, 1746.
Aged 10 mos. & 8 days.

In memory of
DIANAH VAN WYCK,
wife of
JACOB VAN WYCK,
who departed this life
November 28, 1792.
Aged 34 Years & 11 months.

In memory of
ELIZABETH,
wife of
ISAAC VAN WYCK, Esq'r,
who died
Feb'y the 11th, 1800.
Aged 43 Years & 2 Days.

In memory of
CHARLES YOUNG VAN WYCK,
son of
ISAAC VAN WYCK, Esq'r,
& ELIZABETH, his wife,
who died
April 10, 1798.
Aged 1 Year & 15 Days.

WILLIAM VAN WYCK.

Hier Leydt Begraven
CORNELIUS C. VAN WYCK,
overleden De 15th Maert,
Anno 1767. Oudt Zynde
34 Jaar., 3 maanden
en 6 Daagen.

Glory to God alone.
Sacred to the memory
of
ISAAC VAN WYCK.
He was born October 27, 1755,
and departed this life Aug. 28, 1811.
Aged 55 Years, 10 months, and 1 day.

Hier Leydt
Begraven het Lichaam,
Van ANTIE VAN WEYCK.
Overleden den 22d Maert
in t' Jaar Onses Heere
1784. Oudt Zynde
6 Jaar., 2 maanden,
22 dagen.

In memory of
DIANA HASBROOK,
wife of
THEODORUS VAN WYCK,
who died
Oct. 26, 1848.
A E. 81 yrs., 7 mos.
& 3 dys.

Here lyes the Body of
CORNELIUS VAN WYCK,
who departed this life
The 28th Day of June, 1761.
Aged 67 Y., 2 M. & 7 Days.

Here lyes the Body of
HANNAH THORN, wife of
CORNELIUS VAN WYCK.
Was born February the 28th, 1700.
Who departed this Life
Aug. 23, 1771.   Aged 71 Years,
5 months & 23 days.

Hier Leydt Begraven
Het Lichaam van
THEODORUS VAN WYCK,
Soon van CORNELIUS.
Gestorven den 3d October,
Anno 1754.
Out Zynde 54 Yaar., 4 maande, 18 Daagen.

Hier Lydt Begraven
KATHELYNA ADRIEJANSE,
Huis vrow van THEODORUS
VAN WYCK.   Gestorven
De 24 Juny, 1746.
Oudt Zynde 20 Jaar.,
11 maande.

JOSEPH I. VAIL,
Died Dec. 31, 1835.
Aged 68 yrs., 3 mos., 26 days.

DEBORAH,
wife of
JOSEPH I. VAIL,
Died July 19, 1857.
Aged 79 years, 7 mos., 20 days.

SALLY ANN,
wife of
Wm. R. Vail,
Died April 13, 1842.
Aged 35 Years.

PLATT VAIL,
Died Dec. 30, 1846.
Aged 27 Years, 9 months,
23 days.

Hier Leydt Het Lighaam van
JACOBUS VAN NESTE, Bediensat Des
Heylige Evangelimus of Pockkeepsie
En De Viskill, In Dutchess County.
Zynde In De Heere Gerust De 10
April, 1761. Oudt Zynke 26 Jaar.,
2 maande. en 3 Daage.

In memory of
ANNA MARIA VERPLANCK,
who departed this life
October 20, 1779.
Aged 50 years.

In memory of
GERTRUDE VERPLANCK,
who departed this life
the 24th of June, 1794.
Aged 62 Years, 7 months
and 7 days.

In memory of
EFFIE VER PLANCK,
wife of
Philip Ver Planck, Esqr.
Was Born the 16 of February, 1737,
and Departed the Life
November the 22d, 1775.
Aged 38 Years, 9 months
and 6 days.
John Zuricher, stone cutter,

In memory of
PHILIP VERPLANCK, Esqr.,
who departed this life
June 20, 1777.
Aged 40 Years.

In memory of
WILLIAM BEEKMAN VERPLANCK,
who departed this life
30th December, 1804.
Aged 34 Years, 9 months & 28 days.
also
MARY ANN CATHERINE,
Daughter of the above,
who died the 19 July, 1804.
Aged 4 Years, 11 months & 26 days.

MARGARET VERPLANCK,
wife of
PETER MESIER,
Died
Nov. 7, 1852.
A.E. 81 yrs., 2 mos.

In memory of
WILLIAM VERPLANCK, Esqr.
Born the 28th Day
of March, 1693,
and died the 6th day of
June, 1745.

HENRY D.,
son of
STEPHEN B. & SUSAN WALDRON,
Died Nov. 17, 1821.
Aged 10 mos., 5 days.

HANNAH,
wife of SAMUEL WALDRON,
Died Feb. 25, 1803.
Aged 59 years, 5 months.

STEPHEN B. WALDRON,
Died March 7, 1850.
Aged 57 yrs., 4 mos., 7 d'ys.

SUSAN,
wife of
STEPHEN B. WALDRON,
Died Feb. 28, 1872.
Aged 82 yrs., 11 months, 16 days.

ALLETTA MARIA,
Daughter of
STEPHEN B. & SUSAN WALDRON,
Died Aug. 23, 1849.
Aged 30 yrs., 1 mo., 16 d'ys.

CHAUNCY WEEKS,
Died Dec. 6, 1837.
Aged 64 years, 1 mo., 28 dys.

JAMES WEEKS,
Died Aug. 31, 1848.
Aged 66 years, 7 mos.

SALLY,
wife of
JAMES WEEKS,
Died Sept. 30, 1848.
Aged 69 yrs. & 5 months.

JOHN G.,
son of
JAMES & SARAH WEEKS,
Died Dec. 6, 1843.
Aged 31 yrs., 7 mos.

RICHARD WEEKS,
Died May 8, 1842.
In the 41st year of his age.

LETITIA WEEKS,
wife of
RICHARD WEEKS,
Died Dec. 3, 1846.
Aged 44 Years.

ISAAC,
son of
RICHARD & LETITIA WEEKS,
Died May 3, 1854.
Aged 19 Years.

GEORGE,
son of
RICHARD & LETITIA WEEKS,
Died Dec. 14, 1841.
Aged 18 yrs., 2 mos.

GILBERT WEEKS,
Born April 27, 1741.
Died March 12, 1799.

JEMIMA WEEKS,
Born June 21, 1746.
Died June 27, 1808.

RICHARD WEEKS,
Died Dec. 2, 1833,
In the 64th year of his age.

NANCY,
wife of
RICHARD WEEKS,
Died Aug. 16, 1838.
Aged 66 Years, 2 months.

ADELINE,
Daughter of
SALLY and JOHN V. WEEKS,
Died Oct. 9, 1822.
Aged 2 Years.

PHILIP,
Son of
JOHN V. & SALLY WEEKS,
Died Nov. 16, 1833.
Aged 2 yrs., 9 mos., 7 dys.

JAMES WEEKS,
Died Nov. 15, 1790.
Aged 53 Years.

GEN. FREDERICK WESTBROOK,
A Patriot & Soldier of the Revolution,
Died Dec. 6, 1827.
Aged 74 Years.

HANNAH WESTBROOK,
wife of
CORNELIUS D. WESTBROOK
& daughter of ISAAC VAN WYCK.
She died on the evening of the
Lord's Day, the 23d Feb., 1817,
In the 30th year of her age.

MARIA,
wife of
MARTIN WILTSIE,
Died May 6, 1808.
Aged 37 Years, 9 mos.

ANN HUMPHREY,
wife of
MARTIN WILTSIE,
Died Apr. 14, 1775.
Aged 42 Years, 1 month.

WILLIAM WILEY,
Died July 8, 1845.
Aged 50 Years, 4 mos., 28 days.

JACOB C.,
son of
F. B. & C. A. WELLS,
Died July 5, 1863.
AE. 11 Days.

HENRY WOOD,
Died Nov. 19, 1852.
AE. 52 Years.

BARTOW WHITE, M.D.,
Born
Nov. 7, 1776.
Died
Dec. 12, 1862.
Aged
86 years, 1 mo.,
5 days.

ANNE,
wife of
Bartow White,
Born
Sept. 14, 1783.
Died
Feb. 5, 1861,
In her 78th Year.

ELIJAH WINTER,
died
July 22, 1857.
Aged 66 Years.

GERTRUDE ARCHIBALD,
wife of
Elijah Winter,
Died
May 26, 1859.
A.E. 65 yrs., 8 mos., 8 d'ys.

ISAAC C. WINTER,
Died
Jan. 29, 1854.
A.E. 28 Yrs., 11 mos.,
24 days.

ENOS WRIGHT,
Born April 15, 1772.
Died June 17, 1855.
In the 84th Year of his age.

ABIGAIL WHITTEMORE,
wife of
ENOS WRIGHT,
Died July 25, 1862.
In the 75th Year of her age.

JOSIAH W.,
son of
ENOS WRIGHT,
Died Sept. 20, 1840.
Aged 19 yrs., 2 mos., 18 d'ys.

AMBROS WRIGHT,
son of
Enos and Abigail Wright,
Died March 16, 1848.
Aged 20 Years.

WALTER WRIGHT,
a native of Ettrick Forrest,
Scotland,
Died in this village
June 29, 1840.
Aged 77 Years.

CPSIA information can be obtained at www.ICGtesting.com
Printed in the USA
LVOW07s1608301115

464710LV00034B/2091/P